ENC ESSENTIALS

Getting Started with
Electronic Navigational Charts

David Burch

STARPATH

ISBN 978-0-914025-77-1
Published by
Starpath Publications
3050 NW 63rd Street, Seattle, WA 98107

www.starpathpublications.com

10 9 8 7 6 5 4 3 2 1

Contents

IMPORTANT NOTE

Every effort has been made to confirm the veracity of the content of this booklet. This is, however, a broad subject, open to interpretation in some cases, and potential errors in all cases. The author and publisher cannot warrant it is free of errors or omissions.

The book includes symbols and explanations used on electronic navigational charts, but it does not provide an exhaustive representation of all scenarios that might be encountered.

Preface

By the end of 2024, Electronic Navigational Charts (ENC) are projected to be the only official NOAA charts. As of August, 2023, over 60% of all traditional NOAA paper charts have been discontinued, and hundreds of new ENC have replaced them. ENC are already common on commercial vessels using ECDIS (electronic chart display and information systems), having been available for over twenty years, but for recreational mariners, ENC are still rarely used.

This booklet is intended to provide the information needed for all mariners to get started using these powerful electronic charts successfully, as they will soon be what we mean when we say "nautical chart."

Although they have been in use for many years, ENC are dynamic products, undergoing significant improvements as we speak—transitioning from legacy ENC to reschemed ENC. As such, many commercial mariners will be continuing to learn about the format and full functionality of ENC alongside recreational mariners being introduced to them for the first time. Our hope is both groups can benefit from ENC status and procedures included here.

Sources for products and services mentioned in the text are in the References section.

Acknowledgments

I would like to thank Tobias Burch for his work on the graphics, design, and editing of this booklet. We have benefited over the years from the use of several navigation programs listed in the References and remain grateful for the opportunity to use these fine programs. Extended discussions about ENC with Philippe Lelong, developer of qtVlm, have been both productive and enjoyable. Thanks to Andrew Haliburton, navigator of the division-winning Zero Gravity in the 2023 Transpac for ongoing discussions of yacht racing navigation and the powers of Expedition. Proof reading with suggestions from Starpath instructor Dave Wilkinson have been helpful, as they always are. Thanks Dave.

The ENC development team at NOAA offer ongoing and invaluable support on all matters of ENC. Reach this excellent resource through their online AS-SIST program.

1. What is an ENC?

ENC are vector charts that differ notably from *raster* navigational charts (RNC), which are static graphic images of the corresponding paper charts. Vector charts are basically a mathematical set of drawing instructions that tell the display software how to create the chart drawing based on user selected options, such as zoom scale, contour choices, symbol styles, level of detail, among others that we explain this booklet. The ENC in view is created on the wing every time we load it or change its perspective by zooming or panning. Usually this is accomplished very quickly, so this creation process is not discernible.

Since ENC are effectively digital layers of information, they can contain many more specific details about individual charted objects than a paper chart can. Their appearance and display behavior, however, differ notably from what we are accustomed to with traditional paper charts, so their acceptance among recreational mariners has been slow. The symbols are different and their size on the screen does not change with zoom level. There are prominent new symbols that appear in some cases and not others. Also, the charting of land areas on ENC is notably more sparse than on paper charts, which is rightfully distracting to many, even knowing that NOAA is in the process of improving that coverage.

The reluctance to adopt ENC has likely been a matter of training in many cases; once we learn how to use them, most mariners recognize the efficiency, thoroughness, and convenience of the presentation. After all, many mariners are already accustomed to using third party vector charts in their GPS chart plotter displays. The only difference is the ENC are official charts, updated weekly, with much more information, standardized display formats, and fewer errors. Plus, essentially all available navigation programs that can display ENC, even those that are free, include much enhanced functionality compared to typical chart plotters.

It is important to stress that the name *electronic navigational chart (ENC)* is a legally defined term that refers only to charts that meet the International Hydrographic Organization (IHO) chart standard S-57. This specifies what objects are to be included in the chart, and what attributes that describe these objects are to be included, along with the standardized names of each. It also establishes the categories of the objects.

Third party vector charts are not ENC, and apps that use them require an end user license agreement (EULA) wherein the user acknowledges, in one form or another, that they know the charts being used are not official charts, and that official charts are required for safe navigation. There are countless examples that show the importance of that EULA.

Since ENC will soon be the only official charts, it is crucial to have a system at hand that will display ENC. Beyond the safety factor, ENC will be the only way to meet chart carriage requirements that might apply to your operations. Some insurance companies, for example, require official charts on board for some waters, and third-party charts do not suffice.

There is even a proposed new USCG Ruling that will require all operators of commercial vessels, regardless of size, to have some means of displaying ENC. It is not clear yet how this will end up, but as it reads now, if your activity, such as teaching sailing on the water or running chartered fishing trips, requires a USCG license, then this ruling applies to you. Section 3 shows easy ways to meet these requirements.

Existing NOAA chart types are summarized in Table 1-1. See links to viewing each of these online at starpath.com/getcharts. Samples are shown in Figure 1-1.

Table 1-1. Summary of NOAA Nautical Charts	
Traditional paper charts	Starting with 1,220 paper charts in 2019, when their planned demise was announced, we are now (at the end of 2023) down to a total of 484 paper charts still being produced by NOAA. These will be gone by the end of 2024.
Raster Navigational Charts (RNC)	These are the electronic charts made from the graphic images of the paper charts. There is one to one correspondence with the paper charts, and they are identical to them. They will be discontinued as the corresponding paper chart is discontinued.
Electronic Navigational Charts (ENC)	Though in use for many years, the improved versions of these are the charts of the future. As it stands now, ENC are the only official charts for many regions and will be exclusively so at the end of 2024.
NOAA Custom Charts (NCC)	This is an all new concept in nautical charting. It is a way to make a back up (unofficial) paper chart from existing ENC data using an online NOAA app that creates a high res PDF of a user selected region of interest, chart scale, and paper size. See starpath.com/NCC for a portal to related resources.

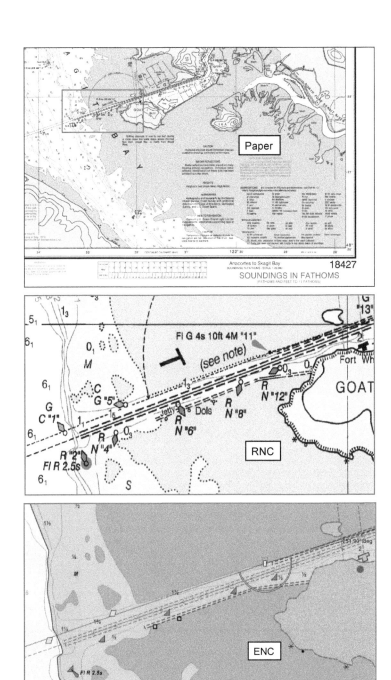

Figure 1-1. *A segment (red) of a paper chart (top), shown as an RNC (middle), and ENC (bottom). The RNC display is identical to the paper chart. The ENC is a vectorized presentation. Notable distinctions include customization of the ENC display regarding depth contours, labels, boundary and symbol styles, and more, along with much less terrain details on the ENC, although this is planned to be improved.*

2. Chart Numbers, Boundaries, and Sources

Regarding chart numbers and boundaries, we must distinguish between *legacy* ENC (meaning those in use for many years) and the new *reschemed* ENC that are slowly replacing them. Unlike paper charts around the world, the ENC chart numbering system is an international standard, which is a key advantage of ENC in its own right. ENC numbers have 8 characters, with the first two being the country of origin code, the next one being the *scale band* of the chart, and the last five being the unique identifier of that chart. For NOAA charts the system of unique identifiers changes with the new reschemed charts. Other aspects of that transition are explained in Section 10.

Here are the samples shown in Figure 2-1:

```
US5CA76M = NOAA legacy ENC chart number
    US = country code
    5 = scale band
    CA = state
    76 = chart ID (Usually no fixed association to adjacent charts.)
    M = filler (All NOAA legacy charts end in M to make 8 characters.)

US6LGBCD = NOAA reschemed ENC chart number
    US = country code
    6 = scale band
    LGB = local region ID (i.e., Long Beach)
    CD = row and column ID among the local set of charts.
```

Scale Bands for ENC				Country Codes	
Bands		**NOAA ENC**		**Code**	**Country**
Scale	*Usage*	*Legacy Ranges*	*Reschemed Values*	CA	Canada
1	Overview	1:10,000,000 to 1:587,870	1:5,120,000 or 1:2,560,000	FR	France
				GB	UK
2	General	1:1,534,076 to 1:240,000	1:1,280,000 or 1:640,000	AU	Australia
				BR	Brazil
3	Coastal	1:600,000 to 1:150,000	1:320,000 or 1:160,000	CL	Chile
4	Approach	1:150,000 to 1:25,000	1:80,000 or 1:40,000	DE	Germany
				EG	Egypt
5	Harbor	1:51,639 to 1:5,000	1:20,000 or 1:10,000	ES	Spain
				NZ	New Zealand
6	Berthing	1:12,000 to 1:2,500	1:5,000	US	USA

Figure 2-2. *ENC scale bands and sample of country codes. ENC usage descriptors are similar but not identical to those describing paper charts. There are 86 nations with Hydrographic Offices that produce ENC. Note ranges vs. specific values on the scales.*

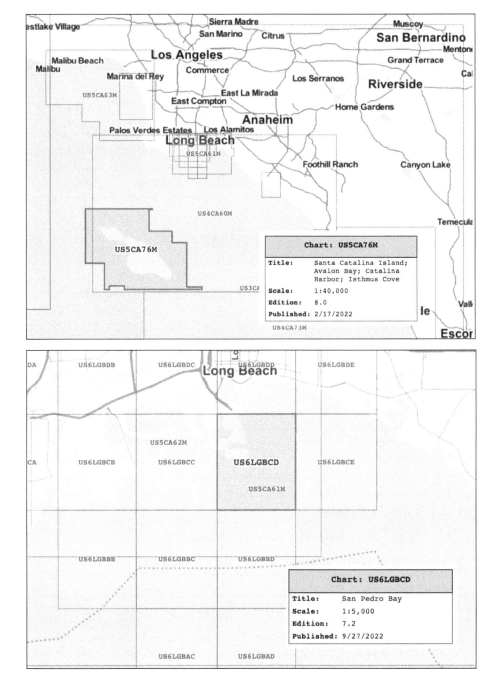

Figure 2-1. *From the Chart Locator at charts.noaa.gov, showing both legacy and re-schemed ENC. The former typically have irregular borders, whereas the latter have regular, consistent sizes. In the top we see highlighted a scale band 5 legacy chart with scale 1:40,000, consistent with the broad range of scales it could be; in the bottom is a scale band 6 reschemed chart with the 1:5,000 that it must be. See Figure 2-2. See also starpath.com/getcharts.*

Like paper charts, ENC also have *titles*, not just numbers. Sample titles can be seen in Figure 2-1. All 15 of the 1:5,000 reschemed charts pictured have the same title "San Pedro Bay." NOAA also refers to the chart *number* as the chart *name*, therefore chart's name and number are the same, but different from its *title*.

The shapes and boundaries of ENC, and the overlap in areas of legacy and reschemed charts, makes for a complex looking chart catalog, but in practice this does not really matter. The file sizes are all relatively small, so the best practice is simply to download and install all of the ENC for the state or states you care about. The viewing software can sort out what you see, at what scale, and all the charts will be quilted together in a seamless manner. All nav apps let you choose to show just one chart if you want to, which can be useful in many cases.

Sources of NOAA ENC

NOAA ENC are free and easy to access at charts.noaa.gov, which at present brings up the option "ENC" that lets you download individual ENC by name, state, region, or USCG District or the option "Chart Locator" which is an interactive graphic catalog. State sets vary in size. A larger one is about 30 MB. Or you can download all NOAA ENC in a zip file of 885 MB that expands into 1.4 GB on your hard drive. There are also options to download just charts that are new over the past day or past week, but many popular navigation programs have automated functions that will keep your charts up to date with more or less just a button-click. ENC are updated Thursdays, at about 10 am East Coast time.

With such efficient distribution, there is no reason not to have every chart you might ever possibly need on your computer, or even in your phone. See starpath.com/getcharts for a convenient portal to US and international charts.

Receive NOAA support by phone or their convenient ASSIST app at nauticalcharts.noaa.gov/customer-service/assist.html. This is also a place to report errors or suggest additions.

Sources of International ENC

Links to international charts are compiled at starpath.com/getcharts. Navigators using the free navigation apps OpenCPN or qtVlm have unique access to economical official ENC that work only on these respective programs. See o-charts.org for the former and meltemus.com for the latter. Other popular nav apps such as Expedition, Coastal Explorer, and others, offer direct purchase of third-party international vector charts that look and behave very similar to ENC. Coastal Explorer also offers official Canadian ENC. Most international charts are not free. The US and New Zealand are the two notable exceptions. All nations do, however, offer free Inland ENC (IENC) for their rivers, with some coastal estuary coverage. In the US, the Western Rivers are covered by IENC produced by the US Army Corps of Engineers.

3. How to View an ENC

ENC are files of a specific digital format that can only be viewed in software designed to show them. This can be an online app such as NOAA's seamless ENC viewer, or stand alone navigation programs (nav apps). Many nav apps can do this, but not all. Some nav apps are limited to RNC or to specific third-party vector charts. Most quality commercial nav apps, however, can show ENC, as can two notable free products, OpenCPN and qtVlm.

The NOAA ENC viewer is a good way to have a quick look at any ENC of US waters. Figure 3-1 shows samples.

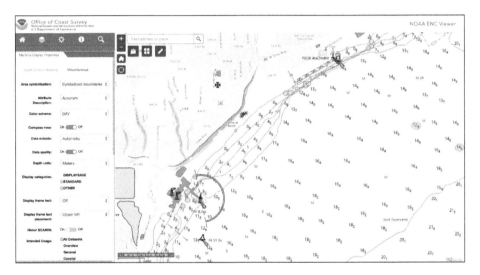

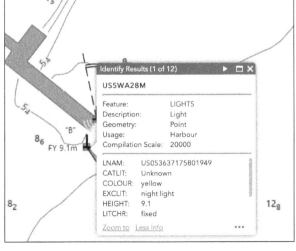

Figure 3-1. Top. *An ENC as seen on NOAA's online viewer. In the left panel, users choose various display options discussed in later sections. The viewer offers a seamless display of all US ENC. When a chart is identified it can be downloaded from a different NOAA link, although there are better ways to select an ENC.* **Right**. *To learn about individual chart objects, select the info icon and then click the object, as discussed in Section 5. Here we see there are 12 objects at the point clicked, including the light, its beacon, water depth, magnetic variation, the name of the water way, and others.*

The official name of a stand alone nav app that will show ENC and connect to your GPS so your live position is displayed on the chart is *electronic chart system (ECS)*. ECS are distinguished from the ECDIS that are required on large commercial vessels. ECDIS must adhere to the strict display standards set out in the Presentation Library of the IHO standard S-52. Most ECS strive to match the S-52 standards as best they can, but since they are not required to, they can individually decide there are better solutions and use those. Both ECS and ECDIS use the identical ENC file, and all ECDIS will present the chart elements in the same way, but across multiple ECS we will see variations in the presentation. Mariners are free to choose the ECS chart presentation they prefer, but that decision is also strongly influenced by other features and options of the ECS beyond how they display charts.

Going forward, we use ECS to refer to "navigation program," "nav app," "navigation software," etc., as it is the official term; it will likely become more familiar as more mariners move into the use of ENC.

ENC are most commonly viewed underway on a computer screen or tablet. This can be a fine distinction in screen size, comparing a large tablet with a smaller laptop, but there is notable difference in the logistics of the ECS software itself. Mobile apps have higher restrictions on functionality and distribution, and some of the leading commercial ECS do not have mobile versions. Also some of the more popular mobile-app ECS do not have computer counterparts. Again, we refer here only to products that can show ENC, not the many popular products that use unofficial third party charts.

The two leading free computer based ECS, OpenCPN and qtVlm, have mobile versions, but their mobile versions have a modest cost. These two have the advantage of functions and layouts being essentially the same on computers and mobile versions, but with notable differences on how they are executed reflecting limitations of the mobile devices.

The loading and viewing ENC procedure is about the same for all ECS. We download the latest ENC to our computer (or device), and then we tell the ECS where we have stored the charts. Then we select in a chart set up or configuration window a few basic display options such as *Show chart outlines* (usually a good idea, at least at first) and *Chart quilting,* on or off, which aligns the charts edge to edge when on, which is the typical choice for most applications. ENC do not have margins like paper charts and RNC have.

Note that when you first load a chart or charts you may not see them on the screen. A common default option of ECS is have the screen open centered on your boat location and the charts maybe elsewhere. With chart outlines on, go to the region of the charts to find the outlines, and then you may also have to zoom in to see the charts. Sample chart outline displays are in Figure 3-2.

With the usual situation of overlapping charts, each ECS has an algorithm they use to decide which chart will be rendered at which zoom level. For a smooth display, it is best to have all charts loaded, not just selected scales. This is rarely an issue with free NOAA ENC, but it can be an issue with third-party vector charts because the chart manufacturers license the charts by scale and

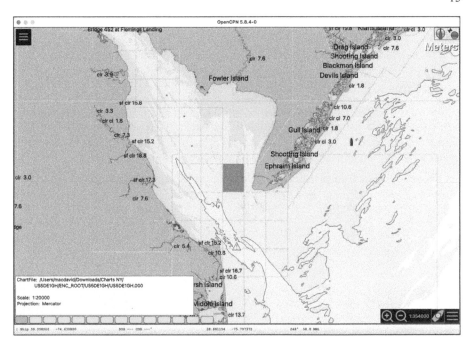

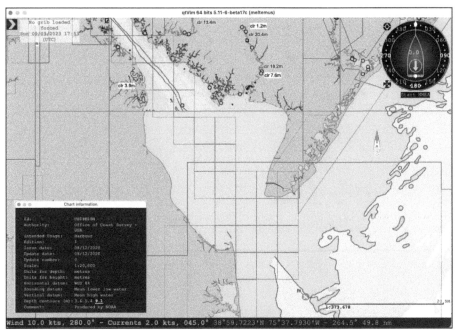

Figure 3-2. *Samples of chart outlines in Base display mode. OpenCPN (top) uses light green for all ENC, with a chart bar button to identify individual charts in view. qtVlm (bottom) shows top layer charts in blue, with larger scale charts behind them in red. Chart info from topmost chart is found from a right-click on the outline. The insert shows the report for the same chart as above, after zooming in until it is on top.*

some apps may choose to not include all scales. This can lead to confusing if not dangerous navigation with those apps.

The two samples shown in Figure 3-2 are using the Base display mode, discussed in the next section, which explains why there are no aids to navigation or other objects shown.

For those new to ENC, one approach is to practice with the two free computer based ECS mentioned, following the basic guidelines presented in this booklet, and then try the several commercial products using the free demo periods many of them offer, and this way decide which you prefer.

There are also free products that display ENC and tell us much about the content of any ENC, but they are not meant for navigation. A notable example is SeeMyENC from SevenCs in Germany.

Figure 3-3 shows samples of ECS and related apps that show ENC.

Figure 3-3. *Samples of ECS and related apps that show ENC. There are numerous others. These are the ones we have used extensively in practice and to prepare this booklet.*

4. Display Modes and Minimum Scales

Unlike paper charts and RNC, ENC offer the user the ability to control how the chart is presented to them. Essentially all ECS adhere to some form of the IHO standard of offering four *display modes* for viewing ENC. A display mode is a selected set of objects to be shown on the screen, as outlined in Table 4-1.

Table 4-1. ENC Display Modes	
Base	Shows bare minimum charting: coastlines, depth areas by color, one safety contour, bridge and cable clearances, and isolated danger symbols. No nav aids (ATONs) are shown. This mode is not intended for navigation. Used sometimes as a background map for viewing tide and current stations or weather overlays.
Standard	Adds to Base most of the objects we would expect on a chart, but leaves off detailed information that is not often needed, such as chart accuracy symbols or inconspicuous objects on land. Standard display would typically be the starting point on using ENC.
All	Is just that; it shows all the objects that are in the chart. It is almost always too cluttered a view for navigation. It does offer a way for a quick check to be sure nothing was missed in an area you care about. All usually disables SCAMIN.
Custom	Activates a list of all objects on the chart with a check box to choose the ones you want to see. After some experience with ENC, it can be a useful way to focus the display on just what you want to see.

The Standard display mode, however, may include more than you want or not all that you want to see. Soundings and depth contours, for example, are not part of the Standard display, but we can add them using one of a series of common ENC display options, shown in Table 4-2.

Samples of the Base display were shown in Figure 3-1. At the end of this Section there are samples of Standard, All, and Custom displays.

Minimum Scale (SCAMIN)

A useful but sometimes challenging option in ENC display is an attribute of every charted object called *scale minimum (SCAMIN)*. At scales smaller than the SCAMIN of an object it will not show on the screen. Thus a special purpose buoy with SCAMIN of 1:44,999 will show on the chart when viewed at a display scale of 1:40,000 and larger, but will not show on, for example, a 1:80,000 display. This can be a useful attribute of ENC objects because of the rule that the size of an object symbol on the screen should stay the same for all display scales, which can lead to a cluttered screen as you zoom out without SCAMIN in effect.

Table 4-2. Display Mode Overrides and Options	
Water depth display	The user has much control over water depth display in ENC. Soundings and depth contours can be turned on or off, depth areas can be presented in 2 or 4 colors, contour labels are optional in many ECS, as is the option to de-clutter or change the size of the soundings. Section 5 covers more options.
ATONs	Major light symbols can be distracting on some scales so they can be turned off as needed, as can the labels and names of most objects on the chart. Thus we can turn them on to identify the objects then turn them off to clean up the chart display.
Symbols	There are usually two choices of symbol styles, traditional or simplified. Purely a matter of personal taste.
Boundaries	Boundaries marking restricted areas, anchoring, dredged, etc., are often crucial to navigation, but they can be cluttering if fully symbolized with their meanings. ENC offer the option to replace the symbolized borders with simple lines.

With that said, however, all ECS have the option to turn SCAMIN off, and this might be the best way to learn the use of ENC. As you notice the need for this attribute, you can turn it back on. Also, several ECS offer the option to scale the sensitivity of the SCAMIN values to meet local needs. With that option you could, for example, change charted 1:44,999 values to not take effect until, say, 1:90,000. Figure 4-1 shows a small scale view with SCAMIN turned off, then in Figure 4-2 we see SCAMIN in effect.

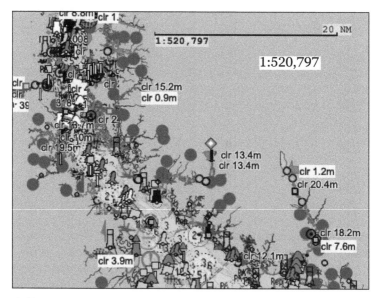

Figure 4-1. *Zoomed out with SCAMIN turned off, charts can be cluttered, but this one would look normal zoomed into actual navigation displays. See also Figure 4-2.*

Table 4-3 summarizes how the view of an ENC can be changed by the user, along with changes that take place automatically, covered in later sections.

Table 4-3. Summary of ENC Display Variations
User Controlled
Display mode: Base, standard, custom, or all.
Water Depths: Choose shallow, safety, and deep contours / Two or four colors.
Region boundary lines: Plain or symbolized.
Toggle on/off: Soundings / Chart text (several categories) / Light and buoy labels / Enhanced sector-light display / Cable areas / Plus others... ECS dependent.
Symbol style: Simplified or paper chart.
Automated Changes
Chart in view: Depends on charts loaded, display scale, and ECS policy.
Hidden symbols: Hidden at minimum display scales if SCAMIN option is engaged.
Isolated danger symbol: Appearance depends on safety contour and display mode.
Moving symbols: Prominent region indicator symbols move to best ID the region.

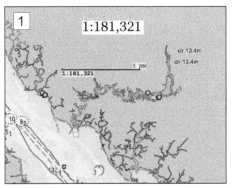
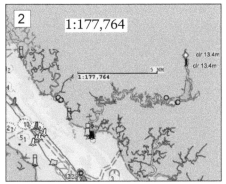
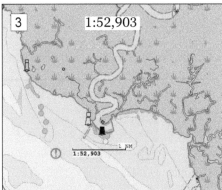
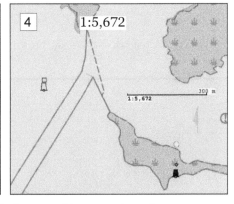

Figure 4-2. *Here SCAMIN is turned on and the buoys and beacons shown have a SCAMIN of 1:179,999. At smaller scale displays (1), we do not see them; at larger scales we do. The marsh symbol on this chart has SCAMIN of 1:59,999.*

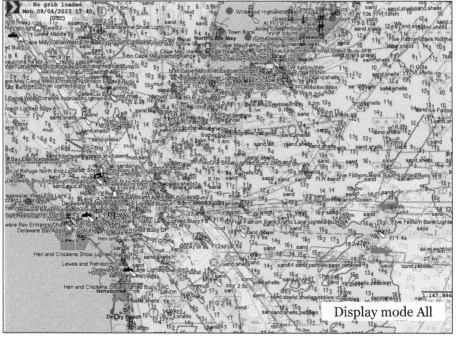

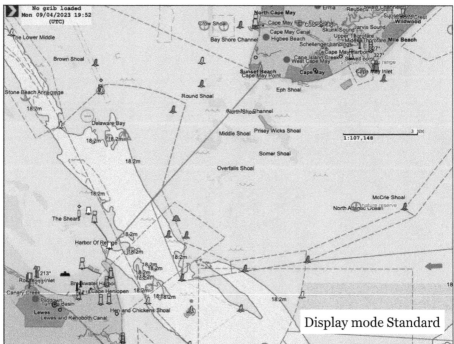

Figure 4-3. *Top shows display mode All; bottom is display mode Standard, with soundings, lights, and ATON labels turned off and boundaries set to plain. Samples of Base display are in Figure 3-1.*

5. Objects, Attributes, and Cursor Picking

Everything shown on an ENC is called an *object*, and each of these objects have a list of properties that describe them called *attributes*. Objects and attributes all have official six-letter abbreviations, which can be useful in some cases, but many ECS avoid them in lieu of the full names.

Using paper charts, we found almost all of what we can know about a charted object from what is printed on the chart. Reference to the *Coast Pilot* can help with landmarks information and the *Light List* almost always helps with extra information about lights and buoys. When we turn to the use of ENC, however, much of that extra information about chart objects is included right in the chart itself. We still want a searchable digital copy of the *Coast Pilot* and *Light List* at hand as they are also primary resources, but we will find much of what we need right in the ENC in the form of attributes.

On a paper chart, we can see the symbol for a light such as shown in Figure 5-1 Left, but if we were sailing near that light in the daylight, we would not know from the paper chart presentation what the light structure looks like if we might want to use it for a piloting fix. We can learn this from the ENC, as well as all the attributes of the light and beacon, and the islet it sits on.

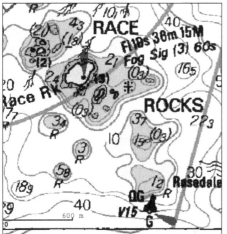
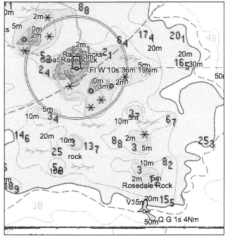

Figure 5-1. Top. *Race Rocks Light house, established in 1860 and manned until 1996.* **Left**. *This is largest paper chart scale for this islet and light.* **Right**. *The corresponding ENC shown at the same display scale, with updated light characteristic—the RNC is old. In Figure 5-2 we zoom in and look at the details of the light and its famous beacon (major tower).*

Using ENC, we learn about charted objects and attributes of the objects from what is called a *cursor pick*, which means putting the cursor on the object and right-clicking—in some ECS this is done with a double-click. This brings up the option to ask for the properties of that point on the chart, which are then presented in a *pick report*. This report tells you about *all* the objects located or in effect at that point, not just the one you clicked.

If we click a buoy, for example, we would learn not just about that buoy, but also the depth information at that location (Section 8), as well as the name of the water way, the magnetic variation at that point, any restrictions in place at that point, and so on. Often the ECS lets the user define the level of detail they want in a cursor pick. We could also, for example, learn the accuracy of the chart at that location, as well as the IALA buoyage system in place. We also learn the minimum scale (SCAMIN) for that object if we have that function turned on.

There is also the option to ask for all related objects at a point, which on a buoy click would bring up any light, fog signal, topmark, racon, or radar reflector associated with the buoy, all of which are independent objects with a list of their own attributes.

When we cursor pick the light from Figure 5-1, for example, shown zoomed in on in Figure 5-2, we would get, among other data, the information shown in Table 5-1, which lists both the abbreviations and the full names of objects and attributes. Although not all ECS use the abbreviations, they can still be valuable to facilitate the use of object catalogs that list all ENC objects along with all the possible attributes of each. See also Figure 5-3 and Table 5-2.

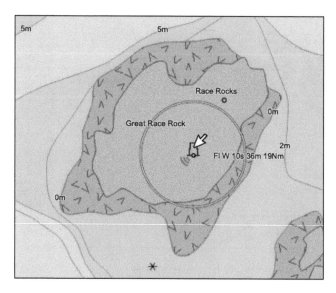

Figure 5-2. *A zoomed-in view of the light shown in Figure 5-1, with a cursor pick (indicated by the arrowhead) that brings up the information shown in Table 5-1, among other chart data related to that location.*

Table 5-1. Sample Cursor Pick Report Components		
Object Light (LIGHTS)*		
Attribute	*Displayed on screen*	*Notes***
COLOR	Color	White	#1 from a list of 13
HEIGHT	Height	118.1 ft	Height above MHW
INFORM	Information	PAC 189	Canadian Light List number
LITCHR	Characteristic	flashing	#2 from a list of 29
SIGGRP	Signal group	(1)	All non-grouped lights use this.
SIGPER	Signal period	10 seconds	Time over which the pattern repeats
SIGSEQ	Signal sequence	00.3+(09.7)	Lighted+(eclipsed) in seconds
VALNMR	Nominal range	19.2 nmi	
Object Fog signal (FOGSIG)		
Attribute	*Displayed on screen*	*Notes*
CATFOG	Category	horn	#10 from a list of 10
INFORM	Information	horn points 155°	A unique detail, not part of a list
SIGGRP	Signal group	(3)	Sounds in groups of 3
SIGPER	Signal period	60.0 seconds	Time over which the pattern repeats
SIGSEQ	Signal sequence	2.0+(3.0)+2.0+(3.0) +2.0+(48.0)	Sounds+(silent) in seconds
SCAMIN	Scale minimum	(40000)	Shows on chart scales ≥ 1:40,000
Object Beacon, special purpose/general (BCNSPP)		
Attribute	*Displayed on screen*	*Notes*
BCNSHP	Beacon shape	beacon tower	#3 from a list of 7
CATSPM	Category	general warning mark	#27 from a list of 56
COLOR	Color	black, white, black, white, black	#1 and 2 from a list of 13
COLPAT	Color pattern	horizontal stripes	#1 from a list of 6
Object Land area (LNDARE)		
Attribute	*Displayed on screen*	*Notes*
OBJNAM	Name	Great Race Rock	International charts have an English and a national language name.

* *Many ECS combine the light information into a custom label that matches what is shown on the chart, in this case: FL W 10s 36m 19Nm.*
** *The number values (#) shown here refer to the item in the official list of attribute values that can be seen in an online object catalog.*

Figure 5-3. *A sample cursor pick and pick report. A simple right-click of this symbol brings up all the information in Table 5-2.*

Table 5-2. Sample Pick Report

US5VA20M   36° 58.260' N, 076° 06.297' W

Buoy, lateral

Shape	Pillar
Category	Port-hand lateral mark
Color	Green
Name	Thimble Shoal Channel Lighted Buoy 7

Light

Color	Green
Exhibition condition	Night light
Characteristic	Flashing
Group	(1)
Period	2.5 s
Sequence	00.3+(02.2)

Restricted area

Information	Regulated navigation area, 33 CFR165.501: Navigation regulations are published in Chapter 2 of the U.S. Coast Pilot for this geographic area.
Restriction	Entry restricted

Navigational system of marks

Marks system	IALA B

Fairway

Name	Thimble Shoal Channel
Traffic	Two-way

Magnetic variation

Reference year	2015
Annual change	-1'
Variation	-11°

Quality of data

Zone of confidence	A1
Source date	20110800
Text description:	US5VA20D.TXT

Depth area

Contours	10.9 m - 36.5 m

Dredged area

Sounding	14.5 m
Name	Thimble Shoal Channel LOQ

Nautical publication information

Usage	Harbour
Compilation Scale	20000
Source date	20110800
Source	US, Chart 12254
Text description	US5VA20A.TXT

Interactive Object Catalog

There are 178 ENC objects and 190 attributes, plus some of these attributes are categories that can have up to 20 possible values (IDs). Each of these objects, attributes and IDs has a definition that is sometimes not so obvious and sometimes important to know. In short, there is a lot more information included in an ENC than we might find in a simple static reference like *Chart No. 1*.

The solution comes in the form of an interactive online ENC Object Catalog, the most dependable of which is a service of the Teledyne Caris Company at

www.caris.com/s-57.

With this service, you find an object alphabetically, then it shows all the attributes that this object might have, then we can click one of those to get its definition or a list of possible values, which in turn have a link to their definition.

Alternatively, you can start with an alphabetical list of all attributes, and work backwards to see which objects might use those. Figure 5-4 is a sample.

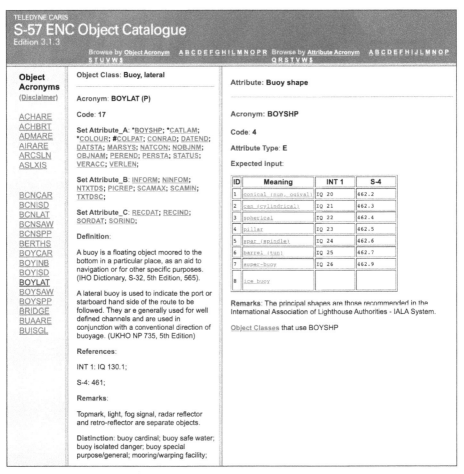

Figure 5-4. *The Caris object catalog, for a Lateral Buoy object (BOYLAT), showing the possible values for the attribute Buoy Shape (BOYSHP), with links to each definition.*

An easy way to practice with cursor picks on an ENC is to use NOAA's interactive, seamless ENC viewer, as shown in Figure 5-5. With that you can look at any object on any NOAA ENC.

Or better still to get started, download one of the free ENC capable ECS (OpenCPN or qtVlm) and then load a chart such as the one below (US4MA14M). Both ECS offer a way to download a chart from within the program. Then practice cursor picking and interpreting the results, checking back with the online object catalog. Samples are shown in Figure 5-6.

For completeness we note there is a second online ENC object catalog at www.s-57.com. It has a similar layout and functionality, but also lists the objects and attributes by full name as well as abbreviation.

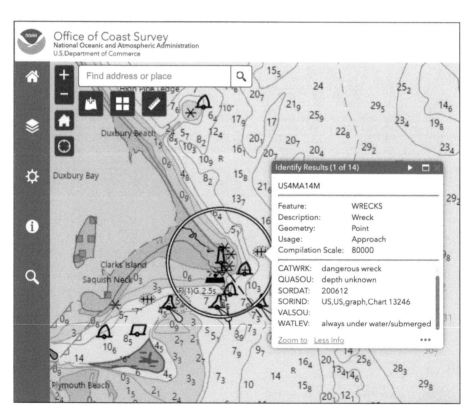

Figure 5-5. *A pick report from the NOAA ENC viewer. At this location there are 14 charted objects to step through with the arrow in the top right of the window.*

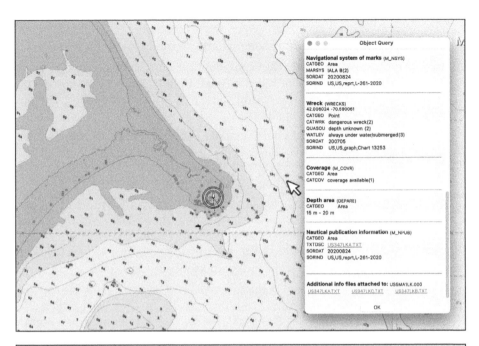

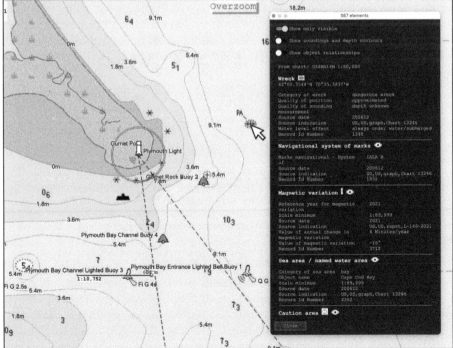

Figure 5-6. *Sample pick reports from OpenCPN (top) and qtVlm (bottom.)*

6. Symbols, Labels, and *Chart No. 1*

ENC users can choose between two styles of symbols, called *traditional paper chart* or *simplif*ied, but the ENC "paper chart" versions are in fact different from what are used on traditional paper charts. Samples are in Figure 6-1.

An immediate stand out are the depth contour labels and soundings, such as shown in Figure 6-2. These are the native soundings on the chart converted to decimal meters. We have the option to display soundings in feet, but the values stored in the ENC are all meters.

The standard reference for chart symbols is a NOAA booklet called *Chart No. 1*, available in PDF. It lists all the actual paper chart symbols with an additional section devoted to what they call "ECDIS symbols." This section could equally well be called "ENC Symbols" or "S-52 symbols."

An enhanced and annotated version of ECDIS Chart No 1 is included in our textbook *Introduction to Electronic Chart Navigation—With an Annotated ECDIS Chart No. 1* listed in the References. Remember, too, that the online ENC object catalogs discussed in Section 5 include definitions of the various objects that can help us learn what the symbols mean.

Beyond stylistic issues, a major change in the ENC symbolism is the consolidation of several previously distinct symbols into one, and we learn which one it represents from a cursor pick. One ENC tree symbol, for example, represents seven different paper chart tree symbols. Rock symbols are also condensed, as covered in Section 7. Also on land, we have multiple landmark objects that were individual on paper charts now condensed on ENC to one symbol that must be cursor-picked for details. Also many paper chart symbols included a label as part of the symbol (i.e., "clock tower," "post office," etc), but these are no longer used in ENC.

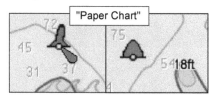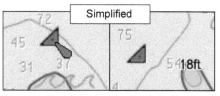

Figure 6-1 *Sample ENC symbols. Left are "paper chart" symbols for a lighted pillar buoy and an unlighted nun buoy. Right are same symbols presented in the "simplified" display choice. Note that the ECS that created these images chose to fill in the red color of the paper chart symbols, whereas the official versions are transparent with black outlines, as seen in Section Q of Figure 6-3.*

Chart Object Labels

Labels on printed charts are static and permanent, with sizes and locations carefully planned. Similar labels on an ENC are dynamic. They can move with display scale, zooming, or panning, but their font size remains the same. Hence there can be congestion and overlap in some displays, which leads most ECS to provide font size and de-clutter options, as well as the option to shut the text labels off completely for some or all objects.

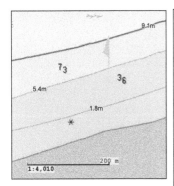

Figure 6-2. Above. *ENC depth contours and soundings in decimal meters. The subscripts means decimal meters. The 5.4 comes from the paper chart origin of 18 ft (18/3.28 = 5.487, which is truncated, not rounded, to 5.4.*

We see these contours:
1.8 = 6 ft
5.4 = 18 ft
9.1 = 30 ft

and these soundings
3_6 = 12 ft
7_3 = 24 ft

Some ECS use the subscripts for the contour labels as well.

Figure 6-3. Right. Chart No. 1 *graphic index to ENC symbols from* Introduction to Electronic Chart Navigation.

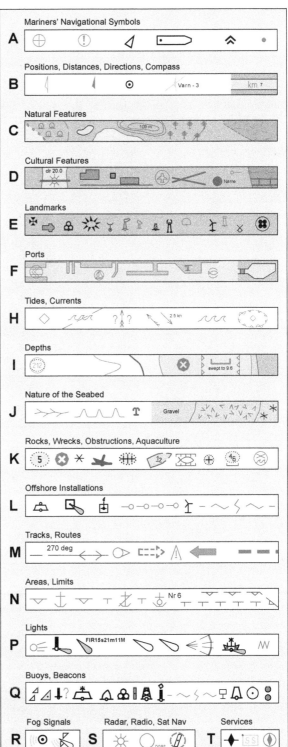

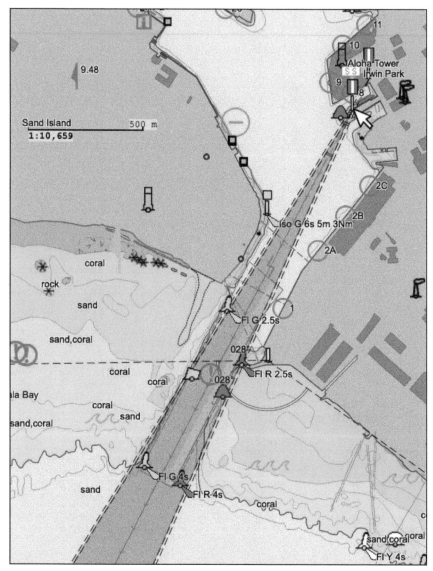

Figure 6-4. *Sample symbols around an entrance range. The cursor over the lead marker triggered an ECS feature of showing the sector light marking the range. Heading in, we see two lighted pillar buoys, then an unlighted can and nun buoy, and two more pillar buoys. Above that is a green light on a beacon with a daymark. There is another (untriggered) green sector light with no label to the right of the second red pillar buoy. This is a 20-nmi major light. The two magenta half arrowheads are magnetic variation symbols. The small one is a spot value of 9.48° E; the large one on cursor pick shows the average over this area. This large symbol is a rare type that moves on the chart depending on your view.*

7. Lights, Buoys, and Rocks

These are three of the major navigation concerns in chart reading, and each has new display features in ENC compared to paper charts.

Lights

The IHO standard on ENC describes lights as the most complex of all ENC objects; rocks, on the other hand, are not complex, but they are crucial objects and their presentation on ENC is notably different from paper charts. Here is a list of unique display issues with lights on ENC.

• All lights can be turned on or off across the chart.

• The names and characteristics of lights can be turned on and off.

• White lights are displayed as yellow, thus without the characteristic showing we must cursor pick a yellow light to learn its color.

• Major lights have a nominal range of 10 nmi or more. Less bright lights are called minor lights.

• Minor lights show a flare symbol as shown in Figure 7-1. If there are two co-located lights, we see two flares.

• Major lights are shown by a prominent full ring, the color of the light (recalling white lights are shown yellow). Since symbols must stay the same size, these rings can clutter the display on small scales. ECS offer various ways to address this, plus the option to shut off the lights. See Figure 7-2.

• The name of a light is more often assigned to the beacon it is on, not the light itself.

• Sector lights show different colors over different bearings. They are used to mark hazards or to guide a vessel along a narrow path. Sometimes they are used to simply mark a line of position where the colors change. These important lights do not have a displayed characteristic label regardless of their brightness (nominal range). See Figures 7-3 and 7-4.

• Obstructed lights are treated as sector lights, and hence do not have a characteristic label. They show a ring sector, regardless of nominal range, and do not show a flare symbol.

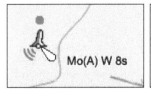  

Figure 7-1. *Sample ENC minor light symbols.* **Left**. *White light on a mid-channel buoy with fog signal and topmark. Topmark and buoy colors added by the ECS.* **Middle**. *Unobstructed minor white light on a special purpose beacon with a daymark.* **Right**. *Red light on a lateral beacon. A cursor pick describes the beacons and daymarks.*

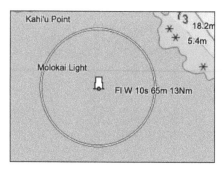 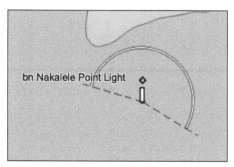

Figure 7-2. Left. *An unobstructed major light shows a full ring and a displayed characteristic.* **Right.** *An obstructed light (major or minor) is treaded like a sector light and does not display a characteristic. We must cursor pick it to learn its properties. This sample is a 6-nmi minor light, which also loses its flare symbol as well.*

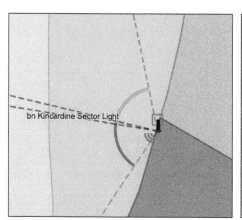 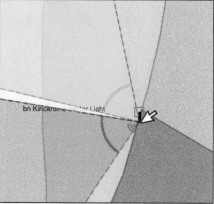

Figure 7-3. *Sector lights can have a name, but will not display a numerical characteristic. Some ECS offer the option to highlight the sectors with a cursor over the light symbol. The sectors extend out to the value of the nominal range.*

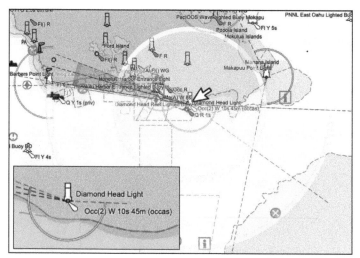

Figure 7-4. *When a sector light shows a flare and characteristic it means there is another light at that location, in this case an emergency backup light, marked (occas) for occasional. Note the different nominal ranges of the lights. Colored lights are usually less bright than the white lights— shown yellow!*

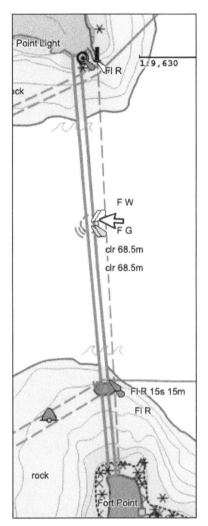

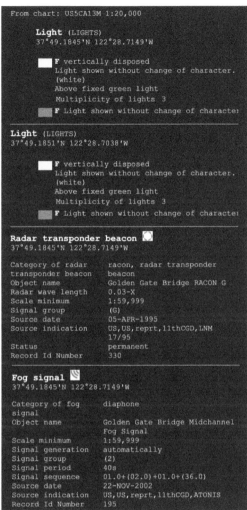

```
From chart: US5CA13M 1:20,000

      Light (LIGHTS)
      37°49.1845'N 122°28.7149'W

         F vertically disposed
         Light shown without change of character.
         (white)
         Above fixed green light
         Multiplicity of lights 3
         F Light shown without change of character

Light (LIGHTS)
37°49.1851'N 122°28.7038'W

         F vertically disposed
         Light shown without change of character.
         (white)
         Above fixed green light
         Multiplicity of lights 3
         F Light shown without change of character

Radar transponder beacon
37°49.1845'N 122°28.7149'W

Category of radar        racon, radar transponder
transponder beacon       beacon
Object name              Golden Gate Bridge RACON G
Radar wave length        0.03-X
Scale minimum            1:59,999
Signal group             (G)
Source date              05-APR-1995
Source indication        US,US,reprt,11thCGD,LNM
                         17/95
Status                   permanent
Record Id Number         330

Fog signal
37°49.1845'N 122°28.7149'W

Category of fog          diaphone
signal
Object name              Golden Gate Bridge Midchannel
                         Fog Signal
Scale minimum            1:59,999
Signal generation        automatically
Signal group             (2)
Signal period            40s
Signal sequence          01.0+(02.0)+01.0+(36.0)
Source date              22-NOV-2002
Source indication        US,US,reprt,11thCGD,ATONIS
Record Id Number         195
```

Figure 7-5. Above. *Example of special bridge lights and the corresponding pick report. There are 3 fixed white lights over a fixed green light on each side. On a paper chart, these light symbols are not shown at all; they are only discussed in a text chart note.*

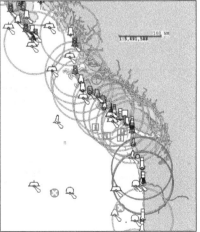

Figure 7-6. Left. *Small scale view of ring symbols for major lights. For chart work at this scale, the lights can be turned off so they do not distract.*

Buoys

• Lights and sound signals on a buoy are considered separate objects. There are no "lighted bell buoys," there are lights, buoys, and fog signals. A sample is in Figure 7-1.

• The characteristic of a light on a buoy is part of the buoy label, but the characteristic of a fog signal on a buoy is not part of the label. We have to recognize the fog signal symbol and cursor pick it for its characteristic.

• Many ECS offer the option to display all related objects in the same display. With this option on, cursor picking the buoy would bring up the list of all related objects, such as: buoy, light, fog signal, day shape, and radar reflector. Otherwise we must click the individual subtle parts of the symbol to get this important information.

• The nominal range of lights on buoys are mostly known and given in the *Light List*, but NOAA does not include these ranges in ENC, although other nations do so. Reasons for this are unclear.

• Spar and pillar buoys, especially in the simplified version, are very similar to beacon symbols, so they are shown tilted as if in a current, whereas beacons are always fixed to land and vertical. Samples are in Figure 7-7.

Rocks

• Rock awash has a new definition in ENC. On paper charts, "rock awash" means it covers and uncovers with the tide, meaning it has a drying height that is between 0 and MHW. On a paper chart, the symbol is a simple asterisk. On ENC, "rock awash" means the drying height is near 0, meaning its top is just at water level when the tide height is 0. On a paper chart, this would be represented by a plus sign with a dot in each quadrant. Both of these rock types are represented by a simple asterisk symbol in ENC. See Figure 7-8.

• Underwater rocks, shown on paper charts as a plus sign, or plus sign with dotted circle to signal known dangerous ones, are all marked with a plus sign and dotted circle on ENC if the sounding is unknown, or a dotted circle with the sounding inside of it when it is known.

• Rocks with unknown soundings or soundings less than the requested safety contour are shown as an isolated danger symbol when on the deep side of the displayed safety contours. Depth contours are discussed in Section 8.

• Important rule: every rock symbol near our intended track must be cursor picked to learn its properties.

Beacons		
Paper Chart	Simplified	Simplified Symbol name
⊥	▯	Isolated danger beacon
	▮	Major lateral beacon, red
⬇	▯	Major lateral beacon, green
	▯	Minor lateral beacon, green
⌂	▮	Major safe water beacon
	▮	Minor safe water beacon
▲	▯	Major special purpose beacon
	▯	Minor special purpose beacon

Buoys		
Paper Chart	Simplified	Simplified Symbol name
⌂	◿ ◺	Conical buoy
⊡	◆ ▱	Can buoy
⌂	⊙	Spherical buoy
⌂	▯	Pillar Buoy
↓	▯	Spar Buoy

Figure 7-7. *Buoy and beacon samples, from Chart No.1, ECDIS symbols.*

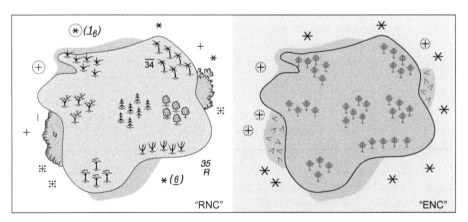

Figure 7-8. *Rock and terrain symbols are greatly simplified on ENC charts. Left is a hypothetical paper chart; right is the corresponding ENC. Six paper chart rock symbols are covered with two ENC symbols, with detailed attributes found by cursor pick. The attractive but challenging tree symbols on paper charts are replaced with a generic tree and a cursor pick. Likewise, coral and rock, represented differently on paper charts, must be distinguished by a cursor pick on ENC.*

8. Water Depths and the Danger Symbol

An important part of ENC set up is the user's choice of displayed depth contours, including selecting one to serve as a *safety contour*, whose choice has several significant consequences. The user can define three contours.

User Selected Depth Contours	
Shallow contour	Is that depth that you will for certain go aground. It would be your deepest draft plus consideration for possible negative tides.
Safety contour	This contour marks the boundary of your guaranteed safe water. As long as you stay on the deep side of that contour, you have no risk of running aground. This would be your deepest draft plus an under keel clearance factor that is your required safety margin.
Deep contour	This is a less crucial choice that can be set to meet a specific navigational need, and indeed changed as needs change. It could, for example, mark a contour you wished to follow as a route; or used to mark deepest waters you could anchor in, or choose it to highlight the bathymetry of the waterway.
Safety Depth	
Safety depth	This is a numerical value, not a contour on the chart, whose primary purpose is to control the color of soundings. Soundings shallower than the safety depth are black, those deeper than the safety contour are gray. This is a valuable setting as we must sometimes sail within the safety contour, as noted below, and this way we can see safe water by the color of the soundings. The safety depth is usually set to equal the value of the safety contour, and with that practice in mind, some ECS do not include a separate safety depth input and instead change the sounding's color at the requested safety contour value.

Choosing the Contours

There is an important nuance to choosing the depth contours you want, especially the safety contour, since it has several special behaviors. The key issue is any of our chosen contours must be native contours already encoded in the chart. If an ENC includes contours at, for example, 12, 18, 30, 60, and 300 ft and you choose a safety contour at 25 ft, you will not get it, as there is no 25 ft contour in the chart. The request field will maintain the "25" you asked for, but the safety contour displayed on the chart and in effect for other purposes will be the next deeper one, which is 30 ft. This is important to keep in mind, and to check the chart itself to learn the actual value of the displayed safety contour, as explained shortly.

And there is a nuance to the nuance! Because of the way the native feet and fathom contours were converted to the metric values required for the ENC, we cannot ask for a specific contour numerically, even if we know it is there. Thus if we want a safety contour showing on the chart of 30 ft, and we know it is there because we can see it, we have to ask for something just less than that, such as 28 ft. For 18, ask for 16, and so on. This problem is fully resolved in those charts that have been reschemed with metrification (Section 10). This limitation on contour selection also applies to the shallow and deep contours.

Role of the Safety Contour

The safety contour is a key component of ENC usage, especially when the displayed contour is close to our requested contour. It is easy to identify the safety contour. It will be the only bold contour line and there will be distinct change in water colors at that line. If not obvious from nearby soundings, we can cursor pick the contour to read its value. Note that depth contours do have a SCAMIN, if that feature has not been disabled, but the safety contour does not.

All ECS will trigger a warning alarm when your vessel icon (or its COG predictor line) crosses the safety contour. Since we cannot always set the safety contour where we want to, it is not uncommon to have to navigate inside of the safety contour, hence just the warning level alarm. If, on the other hand, the COG predictor line crosses the shallow water contour then a danger alarm is triggered.

Note that since we may not get the safety contour we requested, we have conceptually two safety contours. We have the one we *requested* and the one that is *displayed*, which, if different, would be the next deeper one.

Isolated Danger Symbol

The safety contour is also the key to another unique feature of ENC called the *isolated danger symbol*. This prominent magenta circle with a transparent X in the middle marks rocks, wrecks, and obstructions that are on the deep side of the *displayed* safety contour, but have known soundings less than the *requested* safety contour or have an unknown sounding. Samples are shown in Figure 8-1. This feature is considered an important safety enhancement to ENC usage, but there are other subtle rules on their display and these rules can change with display mode.

Water Colors

A universal option for ENC display is the user choice of a two-color or four-color water display. This is clearly a matter of navigator's preference. The four-color option conveys more information, but there is some attraction to the simplicity of the two-color display. The choice will also likely depend on the bathymetry of the area and distribution of the contours. Samples are shown in Figure 8-2.

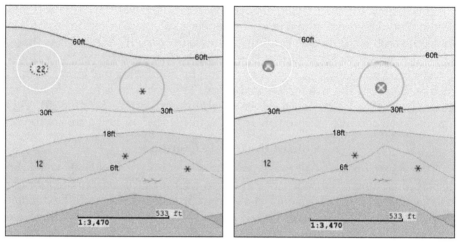

Figure 8-1. *Isolated danger symbols triggered here by an underwater rock with a known sounding of 22 ft (yellow circles) and a rock awash with an unknown drying height (orange circles). These symbols show when the obstruction is shallower than the requested safety contour and outside of the displayed safety contour. On the left the displayed safety contour is 60 ft; on the right it is 30 ft.*

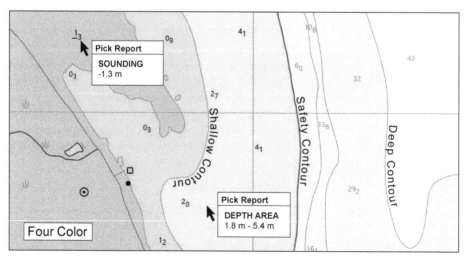

Figure 8-2. *Four-color (above) and two-color (facing page, bottom) water displays. In principle, the four colors are standardized, but in practice they vary from one ECS to the next, sometimes notably. Also shown are several cursor pick reports. The areas can be interrogated anywhere between the contours, but a contour cursor pick must be precisely on the contour line.*

Depth Areas

The area between any two depth contours is called a *depth area*. Every cursor pick report asking for chart information at a specific location will include the shallow and deep sides of that depth area. Some ECS and most ECDIS highlight the depth area surrounding the point of the cursor pick, as shown in Figure 8-3. The depth area of the green foreshore is bounded by the sounding datum on the water side, equal to 0 by definition, and by the height datum on the land side, which is mean high water (MHW) on NOAA charts. Since soundings are positive going down, the MHW going up is presented as a negative value, as seen in Figure 8-2.

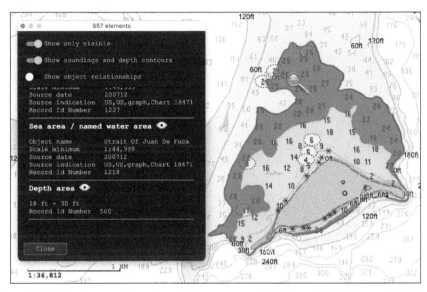

Figure 8-3. *A depth area shown in red after a cursor pick of a point in that area. Only two of the pick report items are shown. The full list covers ten objects at this location.*

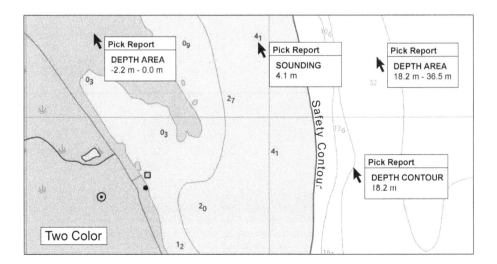

9. Electronic Chart Scales

Chart scale on a paper chart has a simple meaning: a scale of 1:40,000 means 1 inch on the chart represents 40,000 inches on the charted area (about 0.5 nmi). This is a fixed property of paper charts because we view them only at this one scale.

Electronic charts, however, can be viewed at different scales so we need more specific terms. The native, intended-use scale of a chart is called its *compilation scale*. This will generally match that of the paper chart basis of the ENC. The scale of the chart as viewed on the screen is called the *display scale*. Legacy ENC come in many different compilation scales, but when reschemed, there are a maximum of eleven scales and in practice we will be using mostly just four scales.

With a display scale equal to the compilation scale, we should see on a computer screen a good approximation of the intended scale. But when a chart is viewed at a display scale that is larger than its compilation scale, meaning you have zoomed in on it, then that view is called *overscaled* or overzoomed.

Due to the vector nature of ENC, there is a potential hazard to navigating on an overscaled chart, because it will not look distorted, so we have no warning that the chart *at that display scale* may not be as accurate as it appears.

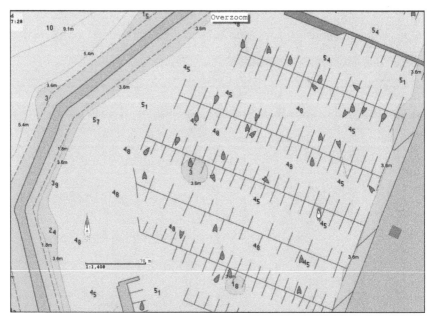

Figure 9-1. *This is a much overzoomed chart, but if we were actually at the location, we could physically see that it was adequately accurate. This could also be concluded from this remote chart view alone, by the locations of the boats that have left their automatic identification system (AIS) transmitters on at the dock. One feature of many ECS is the ability to view AIS signals received from an internet connection.*

Consequently, all ECS implement a required notice to the user that the display is overscaled. The style of the notice varies with ECS. The notice first appears on some ECS at x2 overscale; others do not warn till as much as x4.

There is often call for navigating on an overzoomed chart. An example where it is easy to check the chart accuracy is shown in Figure 9-1. In more isolated waters we must be still more careful, as illustrated in Figure 9-2.

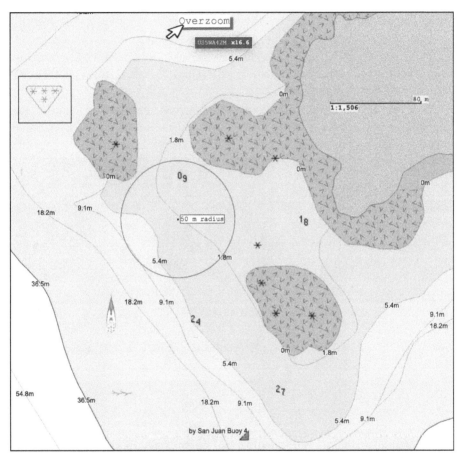

Figure 9-2. *This is a 1:25,000 chart viewed at 1:1,506, which is thus overscaled by a factor of 16.6 (25,000/1,506). This ECS (qtVlm) shows the actual overzoom factor with a cursor on the warning notice. The insert shows the zone of confidence symbol that would be displayed across this chart if we chose to show the Chart Quality object. This symbol (ZOC B) means the location of soundings and contours are accurate to ± 50 m with depths accurate to ± 1 m + 2% of the value. Also added to the image is a mark with a range ring on it with radius of 50 m showing the extent of the chart accuracy. The warning label is a reminder to be very cautious when navigating in close quarters with this type of chart view.*

10. Rescheming, Regridding, and Metrication

NOAA is in the process of making major improvements to all ENC in a program called *rescheming.* This replaces the irregular borders and file names with rectangular borders of fixed aspect and consistent scales with systematic names. Figure 10-1 shows the planned changes. The full rescheming process takes place in two steps. First there is the *regridding,* which establishes the new shapes and sizes, and later the depth contours are converted to metric values that are continuous across the charts. This step is called *metrication.*

Much of the East Coast, Gulf Coast, and Great Lakes, have been regridded, but so far not all have the whole-valued metric contours listed in Figure 10-1. The West Coast has only San Pedro Bay regridded, but plans and schedules are online. A sample is in Figure 10-2.

Figure 10-3 shows chart info displays for two regridded charts, one of which is metrified, the other not. Without such a display option, you can spot which is which by viewing contour labels or cursor picking individual contours. The legacy contours will be standard feet or fathom contours converted to meters and truncated, i.e., 12 ft = 3.6 m, 30 ft = 9.1 m.

Links to rescheming progress and plans are given at starpath.com/getcharts.

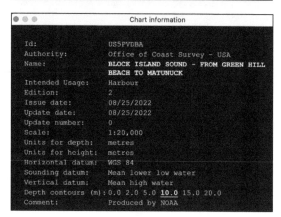

Figure 10-3. *Chart Information displays from qtVlm, which lists the contours contained in each chart, with the safety contour displayed on the chart underlined and bold. The bottom sample has been regridded and metrified, the top is regridded only.*

Properties of Reschemed ENC				
Chart Sizes for Latitude Ranges, w x h (nmi)				Depth Contours (m)
Band	Scale	0° to 49.2°	49.2° to 69.2°	69.2° to 80.0°	
1	5.12M or 2.56M	1152 x1152	2304 x1152	4608 x1152	100 200 300... 50 100 150 200 300...
2	1.28M or 0.64M	288 x 288	576 x 288	1152 x 288	50 100 150 200 300... 20 50 100 150 200 300...
3	320k or 160k	72 x 72	144 x 72	76 x 72	20 30 50 100 150 200 300... 10 15 20 30 50 100 150 200 300...
4	80k or 40k	18 x 18	36 x 18	72 x18	5 10 15 20 30 50 100 150 200 300... 2 5 10 15 20 30 50 100 150 200 300...
5	20k or 10k	4.5 x 4.5	9 x 4.5	18 x 4.5	2 5 10 15 20 30 50 100 150 200 300... 2 3 4 5 6 7 8 10 15 20 30 50 100 150 200 300...
6	5k	2.25 x 2.25	4.5 x 2.25	9 x 2.25	2 3 4 5 6 7 8 10 15 20 30 50 100 150 200 300...

Figure 10-1. *Properties of reschemed NOAA ENC*

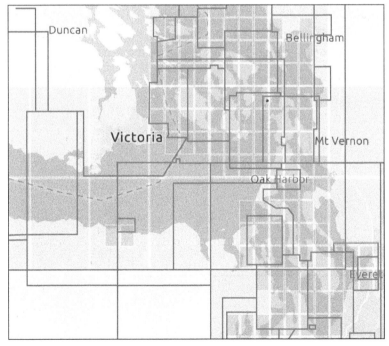

Figure 10-2. *Rescheming plan for part of the Salish Sea in Washington and British Columbia, a 65 nmi span, showing the outlines of the existing legacy ENC in red outlines. This region will be covered by a regular set of 1:80,000 charts (faint magenta) with the indicated blue charts at 1:10,000—legacy ENC in this region span six different scales. This is a big improvement on detail. The best detail now is 1:25,000. The 1:80,000 are planned for 2023; the 1:10,000 dates have not been announced.*

11. Other Benefits of Electronic Chart Navigation

The use of ENC is the foundation for electronic chart navigation, but once this is mastered using any ECS, our focus turns to what other features the various ECS might offer us. There are quite a few powerful tools to consider, and each ECS has their own rendition of them. Below is a brief outline of just a few.

Waypoints and Routes

Although procedures are different, all ECS offer a way to define and store a series of waypoints and then connect them into a route. Beyond that, there are numerous extensions and variations. A sample is shown in Figure 11-1.

With a GPS attached, the ECS knows where you are and knows your speed over ground (SOG) and course over ground (COG), and the ENC in use knows where all the hazards are located. Knowing all that, the ECS can warn you of approaching hazards. Figure 11-2 shows one way this works.

Tides and Currents

A basic ECS feature is the presentation of tide height and tidal current predictions. Almost all ECS offer some way to present the predictions based on harmonic constants available from NOAA or other sources. These data make route planning very much easier than referring directly to NOAA for the data—in 2020 NOAA discontinued the subordinate station correction tables (Table 2), so we must now look up the data for every station we care about. But this ECS convenience includes the obligation to periodically check the data we are getting from the ECS with the official values presented at NOAA. A notable ECS presentation is shown in Figure 11-3.

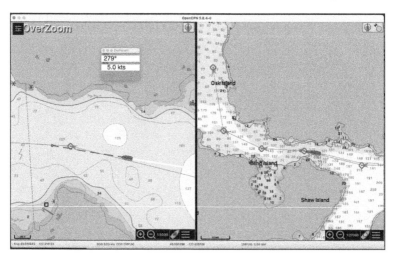

Figure 11-1. *A simple route display in OpenCPN. With its split view you can zoom in to watch the track to see if you are getting set by current, or look for nearby hazards, and in the other window keep perspective on the overview. The route specs can then be exported to a printed route log or imported into mobile devices for backup.*

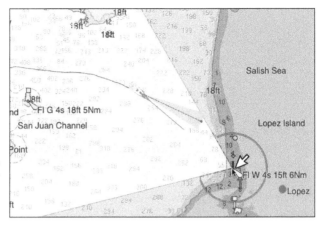

Figure 11-2. *Anti-grounding cone in qtVlm can be set to trigger an alarm at an obstruction or shoaling in time to correct course. This vessel is being set off course by current, which would be noted when the white light turns red—if the cone did not warm them first. TimeZero also has a similar anti-grounding cone option. The location of light color change is displayed when the cursor is on the light.*

Weather Overlays and Sailboat Routing

Most ECS allow for importing wind, wave, or current data to be displayed georeferenced right on the ENC we are navigating with. This is the key to modern navigation, because we can use that data to manually shape a route on our own, or let the ECS compute the optimum route to our destination taking into account these forecasts. Essentially all ECS that use ENC can compute an optimum sailing route. Here we mention just a few of the leading edge data sources and operations.

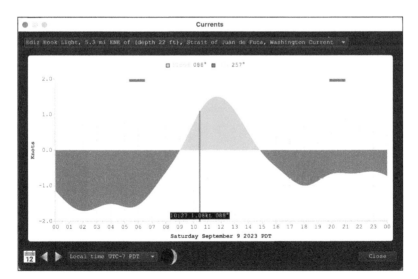

Figure 11-3. *Tidal current predictions from qtVlm. The top dropdown offers the data from other depths at that station. The yellow bar marks the span of daylight with the dark segments marking the twilights. Values at the present time are marked on the plot. The time selector offers local or UTC time, plus station time, which is valuable for planning a route in a different time zone. The calendar button lets you choose any date in the past or future. There is a similar display for harmonic tide predictions.*

A versatile ECS these days also serves as a state of the art weather analysis tool. Figure 11-4, for example, shows recent satellite wind measurements (ASCAT) with an overlay of the GFS model wind forecast at the corresponding time. The ASCAT winds not only tell us what the actual winds are over that region, but they provide a verification of the GFS forecasts that we rely on for the optimum route computations. The data are available globally.

On the leading edge of environmental data technology for inland and coastal waters is the use of tidal current models that give a much more specific view of the tidal current flow over an area than we can get from NOAA's spot station predictions. The data come from NOAA's Operational Forecast System (OFS) model. A sample is shown in Figure 11-5, compared to the relatively sparse data from specific current stations.

The most convenient source of OFS data in grib format is the Mac or iOS weather app LuckGrib. It does not display ENC, but remains a unique source of the best available weather and current data, which can then be exported to other apps as desired. LuckGrib also includes optimum weather routing, and offshore satphone connections, among other attractive features.

Ultimately, the purpose of all the weather and current data we collect is to help us determine the best route to follow in our craft. Sailors know the performance of their boats under various wind conditions (polar diagram) and want to combine that with the wind, seas, and currents forecast to find the optimum sailing route to their destination.

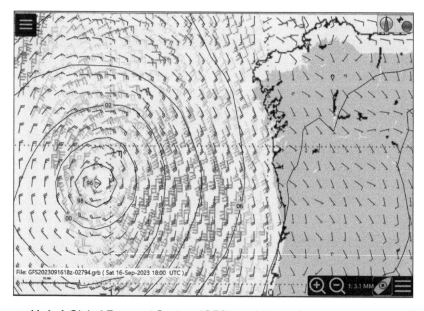

Figure 11-4. *A Global Forecast System (GFS) model wind forecast compared with the actual ocean winds measured by the EUMETSATs satellite borne ASCAT scatterometers. See References for related background links. This OpenCPN example includes a plugin that displays the near live ASCAT data with just a couple button-clicks.*

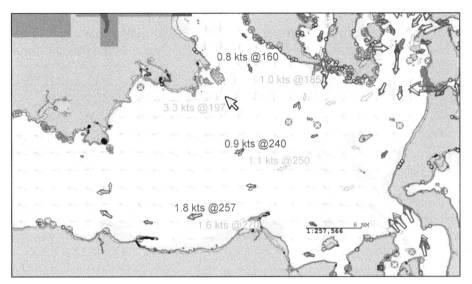

Figure 11-5. *A peek into the future of tidal current studies. OFS model forecasts (green arrows) are compared to NOAA station predictions (outlined arrows, some with multiple depths). The model data are from LuckGrib, displayed here in qtVlm. The model values (green numbers, found from a cursor pick in those areas) are consistent with the spot forecasts (brown numbers), within expected uncertainties, but the model tells us much more than we would know from spot forecasts alone—such as the strong flow at the cursor location. This state of the art tidal current display is easy to implement in any ECS, and can be directly incorporated into optimum routing.*

Essentially all ECS with ENC capabilities offer a way to do optimum sail-boat routing computations, with various levels of sophistication and crucial performance analysis tools needed. The basic requirements for success is a polar diagram that can correctly predict sailing performance for the conditions at hand and, of course, an accurate forecast. If either is wrong, the computed routes could be notably, even seriously, wrong.

Thus it is a process that takes care at each step, including studying various options such as the potential for achieving only some percentage of the antic-ipated performance. Typically new routes are computed several times a day as you learn more about the forecasts and boat performance in conditions at hand.

For the start and finish of an ocean crossing computation, or for many in-land routing tasks, it can be helpful to use real large scale ENC for the back-ground, rather than just a base map that we use in many ocean routing com-putations. This lets the computation navigate around real depth contours so more realistic routing is possible. Without such an option, the user must set minimum distances of approach from the base map boundaries.

An example is shown in Figure 11-6. Rather than just specifying minimum distance from "land," often meaning the base map borders, we can load an ENC and set minimum distance off of the shallow water or safety contour to give more realistic routing near land.

Figure 11-7 is another example of powerful sailboat routing and analysis from the popular racing and performance ECS Expedition. Expedition has the ability to import detailed archived tracks of all boats in past races that were tracked and published live during the race by companies such as ybtracking. com.

As an example, imported YB tracks from a past race (Transpac 2023) for a specific start are imported and compared to computed routes for a boat that took part in the race using reanalyzed GFS winds from that time. The routes are computed for various percentages of polar performance, confirming the navigator's knowledge that downwind he expected to get about 105% of his polar predictions.

This type of analysis can be carried out live during a real race with Expedition, but YB delays the hourly reports by six hours to protect recent maneuvers from competitor's view.

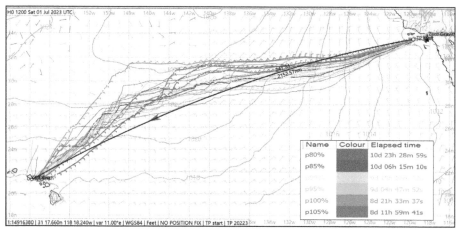

Name	Colour	Elapsed time
p80%		10d 23h 28m 59s
p85%		10d 06h 15m 10s
p95%		9d 04h 47m 52s
p100%		8d 21h 33m 37s
p105%		8d 11h 59m 41s

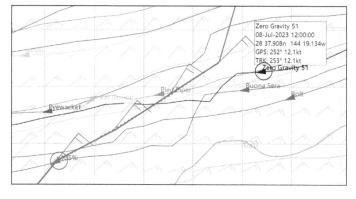

Figure 11-7.
Optimum route computations from Expedition for various percentages of polar performance. About midway, the computed track and actual track are reasonably close considering the many variables unaccounted for.

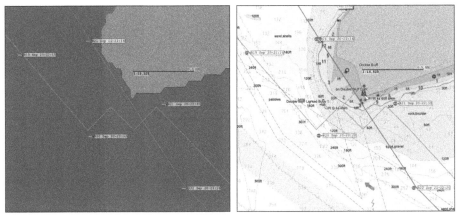

Figure 11-6. *Routing restricted from land (red), which crosses shoal waters, versus restricted to an ENC contour (green). This example from qtVlm restricts routes from crossing the shallow water contour by a safety margin of choice.*

References

• *Introduction to Electronic Chart Navigation: With an Annotated ECDIS Chart No. 1*, (Starpath Publications, 2023). An extended discussion of ENC and navigation using them.

• starpath.com/ENC. This is an extensive list of links to practical matters of navigation with ENC.

• nauticalcharts.noaa.gov. For *NOAA Chart No. 1* and other resources including ENC downloads and support links.

• starpath.com/getcharts. This is an extensive portal to all matters of nautical charts.

• starpath.com/NCC. A portal to all matters related to NOAA Custom Charts.

• View NOAA ENC online with active cursor picks at nauticalcharts.noaa.gov/enconline/enconline.html.

• Sample Electronic Chart Systems (ECS) that show ENC. There are many more, both for computers and mobile devices; these are just the ones we are familiar with and know they present official NOAA ENC that can be updated with files obtained directly from NOAA.

Coastal Explorer	rosepoint.com
Expedition	expeditionmarine.com
LuckGrib	luckgrib.com
OpenCPN	opencpn.org
qtVlm	meltemus.com
SeeMyENC	sevencs.com (viewer only; not ECS)
TimeZero	mytimezero.com

Index

Printed in the USA
CPSIA information can be obtained
at www.ICGtesting.com
LVHW061323221123
764466LV00061B/491